D0628847

The God You Have

FACETS

Selected Titles in the Facets Series

The God You Have

Politics and the First Commandment

Patrick D. Miller

Fortress Press
Minneapolis

THE GOD YOU HAVE

Politics and the First Commandment

"At the Smithville Methodist Church." Copyright ©1986 by Stephen Dunn, from NEW AND SELECTED POEMS 1974-1994 by Stephen Dunn. Used by permission of W. W. Norton & Company, Inc.

Cover design: Ann Delgehausen
Book design: Joseph P. Bonyata

ISBN 0-8006-3662-7

The paper used in this publication meets the minimum requirements of American National Standard for Information Sciences — Permanence of Paper for Printed Library Materials, ANSI Z329.48-1984.

Manufactured in the U.S.A.

08   07   06   05   04   1   2   3   4   5   6   7   8   9   10

Walter Brueggemann

Colleague, Brother, and Friend

Contents

Acknowledgments

This essay is the product of oral and written forays into thinking about the First Commandment. Some parts of it, though now much revised, changed, and expanded, were presented as public lectures at Austin Presbyterian Theological Seminary (Currie Lectures), San Francisco Theological Seminary (Moore), Columbia Theological Seminary (Smyth), United Theological Seminary of the Twin Cities (Gustafson), Anderson School of Theology (Newell), and Central Baptist Theological Seminary (Spring). A shorter form of the present version was given at a colloquium honoring Walter Brueggemann and Charles Cousar on their retirement from Columbia Theological Seminary in 2003 and will be published in a collection of essays in their honor.

The opportunity to talk with colleagues and friends in the course of these presentations means that many persons have contributed to my thinking. I am indebted to all of these but particularly to Wallace M. Alston Jr. and Robert W. Jenson for their helpful comments and suggestions on the present form of the essay and for their general support during my time at the Center of Theological Inquiry in Princeton, New Jersey, where it was prepared.

Once again, I must also express my deepest thanks to President Thomas W. Gillespie and the Board of Princeton Theological Seminary for providing the opportunity to work uninterruptedly on this and other projects during a sabbatic leave. Their unstinting support of faculty research and writing is a great gift to those of us who teach there.

1

The First Commandment as Political Axiom

In 1933, when the Swiss theologian Karl Barth wrote his powerful essay "The First Commandment as an Axiom of Theology," it was a primary weapon in his "fight against natural theology," a fight that he saw as "unavoidable in view of the first commandment as an axiom of theology . . . a fight for right obedience in theology."[1] I would like to suggest that it is also a weapon in the fight for right obedience in politics and against bad forms of political theology. The term "political theology" has valid meanings and uses, in reference both to a powerful theological movement in the second half of the twentieth century and to the fact that theology, if it is talk about God, is thoroughly political in that it deals with the governing of cosmos, church, and polities.[2] When I talk about the fight against political theology, I mean resistance to careless or deliberate confusion of what is political and what is theological, manifest in both politicizing theology and detheologizing politics. That occurs in several ways, specifically in the coalescence of God and country, the takeover of the language of faith in the speech of politics, and the confusion of loyalty with obedience. If the First Commandment is an axiom of theology, it is also and necessarily a fundamental axiom of politics for those who claim to stand under and live by these directives.[3]

For Barth, it was crucial to establish what he meant by "axiom." While that is not as critical for this discussion, I join with his understanding of the First Commandment as axiomatic in that it is "a statement which is sufficiently comprehensive and substantial to form the ultimate and decisive presupposition to the proof of all other statements of a particular scientific discipline."[4] In this case, that discipline is theology, as it was for Barth, but it is also politics, both as they come together and as they are confused. From whichever direction one comes, the First

Commandment is axiomatic. It is the basis and starting point for all further inferences and arguments in both theology and politics. One should note further that while Barth's essay is thoroughly theological—and with little or no reference of any sort to politics, to the state, or to contemporary events—it was delivered at the dawn of the Third Reich only a few days after the burning of the Reichstag and just a year before the Declaration of Barmen, the powerful confession of faith by the German Confessional churches in response to the capitulation of the German Christians to the claims of Hitler and Nazism.[5] Halfway between the publication of his essay and the formulation of the Barmen Declaration, Barth, hoping that Reformed and Lutheran Christians could come together despite their differences, wrote these words in a foreword to one of the issues of *Theologische Existenz heute* [Theological Existence Today]: "Today, the conflict in the Church is not over the Lord's Supper but over the First Commandment, and we have to 'confess.'"[6] Then, after having to leave Germany and becoming concerned from afar about what was happening in the Confessing Church,[7] he felt that the Confessing Church had not understood and in part did not even want to understand that the acknowledgement of the first commandment 'under National Socialism is not just a "religious" decision. It is not a decision of church policy either. It is in fact a political decision. It is a decision against a totalitarian state which as such cannot recognize any task, proclamation or order other than its own, nor acknowledge any other God than itself.'[8]

His essay, therefore, should be read and understood in reference to what was going on and what lay just ahead, even as the Barmen Declaration should be read in the light of Barth's "axiomatic" claim.

Further, Barth has only one formal discussion of the First Commandment, "You shall have no other gods but me," in his major work, *Church Dogmatics.* It occurs in his explication of the first article of the Barmen confession, "Jesus Christ as attested to us in Holy Scripture is the one Word of God whom we must hear and whom we must trust and obey in life and in death."[9]

2

What Do You Do with the God You Have?

The issue for God's people is characteristically wrong God and not no God.
                    —Walter Brueggemann[1]

Walter Brueggemann makes an important distinction in the epigraph above. I would go on to suggest that what he says is generally the case for the human community, though it is not up to us to decide that for others. Observing what goes on in our culture, however, we can see that there are few avowed atheists around. Many people are practical or pragmatic atheists much of the time, though even then the reality may be an ignoring of God, an acting as if God does not have to be taken account of except on special occasions—whether those are celebratory and ritual moments, extreme situations (e.g., the foxholes of war), or whatever. Much of the time God does not seem to matter sufficiently for one to be against God. Indifference, I think, is a more common phenomenon than atheism or agnosticism. Both those positions require a more serious engagement with the question.

I propose, therefore, that the fundamental question is not, Do you believe in God, or even in one God? but *What do you do with the God you have*?[2] In one sense, forming the question this way is nonsensical or wrongheaded, particularly if understood to mean that having God implies some kind of power and control. If you assume that, you will find yourself not to *have* God but to have been *had* in the most basic sense one can imagine. It is vital to understand that the whole point of the First Commandment is that before you have God, God has you. The Commandments begin with the Prologue and its implications:

> I am the Lord your God, who brought you out of the land of Egypt, out of the house of slavery; therefore you shall have no other gods before *me* or

make images of anything and you
shall not worship them because *I the*
*L*ord *your God* am a jealous God . . .
(Exod 20:2–5)

These distinct but interrelated statements are held together by the first per-
son speech, the self-referentiality of the
divine word at the beginning. Before the
Commandments open up to the self and
the selves who are addressed, to the per-
son and to the community of persons,
they are self-presentation and self-assertion. They are from God, about God. In
effect, "You have me because I have you."
Eventually you can—and must—turn to
the family, the neighbor. But not before it
is clear that God is given and God is *a*
given, that is, given to you as the liberating Lord and a given that makes it impossible for you to act as if the reality of God
is not before you, behind you, beside you,
over against you, the starting point and
ending point, just as you cannot have any
other gods before me, behind me, beside
me, over against me, no other starting
point or ending point, no other bottom
line.[3] So, since you are so found, caught,
constrained, led, and possessed, what now

will you do with the God you have
because that God has you?

I keep saying "you," but this is not a
homiletical "you." It is the "you" of the
Commandments. I keep saying "you" not
to preach but because that is how the
Commandments speak, that is what they
say; they speak to and about "you" and
they leave open who the "you" is even as
the divine word comes to a very specific
people in a specific time and space, a
moral space forever known as Sinai[4]– not
a generalized space of virtue, but the
meeting of God and the freed community,
who now have this God. The "you" is specific and definite, but it is open and wide.
That is, the "you" is grammatically singu-
lar and so addresses its object, its recipi-
ent, as an individual, as a single human
being; but the "you" is also an address to
a community that stands before its Lord–
an inclusive assembly that hears this individualized and personalized "you" as
addressing it precisely in its completeness
and its wholeness. Each individual as
individual, the whole community as a
group, a people, a worshipping assembly,
etc.–that is the "you" to whom God
addresses this and each commandment.

But the "you" is *open*. When Moses, on the plains of Moab, recalls these words of the Lord at Horeb/Sinai, he makes it very clear to whom they are directed: "Not with our ancestors did the LORD make this covenant but with us, we, these ones, here, today, all of us who are living" (Deut 5:3). "You" cannot get away from that if you try. This, of course, is the danger of the Word, then and now, that one gets trapped in it and can no longer just read and listen but has to say "That's me; this word is for us." "And God spoke all these words" to *us*, the ones who are reading and hearing them right now, to those of us who are living today, to all of us. The "you" of address disappears only at this *one* point—"not with our ancestors"—in order that the "you" addressed—"us, we, these ones, here, today, all of us who are living—can be opened up. We hear these words no longer as words to our mothers and fathers, to our grandmothers and grandfathers, to Calvin and Luther, to Moses and Israel. They are the covenant the Lord has made with those who are right here and right now—with us.

So the "you" is open, not closed, not limited and delimited. It is the "you" whom God has created and the "you" who would be slave to something without the freeing grace of God. It is the "you" gathered before the Word and before the Table, that is, the "you" who meet the Lord in thunder and lightning to hear the Word and be confronted with the awesomeness of God, the "you" who meet the Lord at the holy place and know that they may not survive such a meeting. And it is the "you" who have to swear oaths and tell truths, who have to sign documents and pay taxes and give verdicts and go into debt and take loans and become either poor or wealthy in the process. It is the "you" who have to deal with rebellious children and aged parents. It is the "you" who pick up the sword and lay it down. It is the "you" in the gate, the courtroom, and city hall, because before Sinai is over, the people who have this God have this God not only as a worshipping community but as a polity.

The axiomatic character of the First Commandment, then, is the result of its grounding in the divine self-giving, in the test of who is God and what power is at work in the world—one that embodies oppressive political rule versus one that is wedded to the release of the oppressed and suffering and will not let attachments to lesser entities claim an obedience under the rubric of loyalty. The alternative name for these Commandments (literally "the ten words"—Deut 4:13; 10:4) is "the covenant" (Exod 34:28; Deut 4:13). While the Sinai covenant is rooted significantly in familial and kinship structures, the closest analogies to the biblical covenant have been found in the suzerainty treaties—between vassals and kings—of the ancient Near East. There is much debate about what this means historically, but that is not the issue here. The treaty analogy is indicative of the fact that the very structure of Israel's life as rooted in the Commandments is fundamentally political and one that supersedes and rejects all other possible political structures as having any final claim on those who live in, with, and by this covenant.

3

The Prologue as Political Announcement

The theological claim of the Prologue to the Commandments is a political announcement. Its primary meaning is that those who worship this God do so as people who know themselves to be set free by God's grace and mercy.[1] There is no foundation for the claim and no analogy to it. There is only the story of God's freeing grace and covenanting demand. There are, of course, other stories that the Lord has with other peoples, for the Bible alludes to these. But we cannot know them and so can only live by the covenant made with "us, we here, these ones, living, all of us, here, today" (Deut 5:3).

That *story*, however, is critical. If the First Commandment is the presupposition of theology, as Barth argued, and also the presupposition of politics, which Barth simply asserted and lived and which I am arguing, the story—"I am the LORD your God who brought you out of the land of Egypt, out of the house of slavery"—is the presupposition of the First Commandment. So you live by it because it is your story of freedom and mercy (all of us, here, today, those of us living now) and it is the best story you know. The church has always believed that telling the old, old story is what claims people's lives. "I am the LORD your God, who brought you out of the land of Egypt, out of the house of bondage [the story], *therefore* you shall have no other gods besides me [the claim]."

The truth and power of this story, this whole story, to claim our lives is poignantly attested in Steven Dunn's poem, "At the Smithville Methodist Church," the first part of which is as follows:

It was supposed to be Arts and Crafts
    for a week,
but when she came home
with the "Jesus Saves" button, we
    knew what art
was up, what ancient craft.

She liked her little friends. She liked
    the songs
they sang when they weren't
twisting and folding paper into dolls.
What could be so bad?

Jesus had been a good man, and
    putting faith
in good men was what
we had to do to stay this side of
    cynicism,
that other sadness.

O.K., we said. One week. But when she
    came home
singing "Jesus loves me,
the Bible tells me so," it was time to
    talk.
Could we say Jesus

doesn't love you? Could I tell her the
    Bible
is a great book certain people use
to make you feel bad? We sent her
    back
without a word.

It had been so long since we believed,
    so long

since we needed Jesus
as our nemesis and friend, that we
    thought he was
sufficiently dead,

that our children would think of him
    like Lincoln
or Thomas Jefferson.
Soon it became clear to us: you can't
    teach disbelief
to a child,

only wonderful stories, and we hadn't
    a story
nearly as good.[2]

The theological claim of the Prologue is a political announcement also because those who worship "the LORD your God" know that obedience to this God carries, as Barth put it, no "and" with it.[3] It stands alone. Once the claim that you have this God is made *upon* you—in the Prologue—and taken up *by* you—in the First Commandment—there is nothing you can have alongside this God. For Barth, the fight was over natural revelation, because he saw there the "and" that could produce blood and soil, that could associate God with things that belong to our natural life or to orders of creation. He already knew, however, that this was not simply an inner theological debate. The ground was being laid for an "*and*," something "beside me," beside God and beside what is revealed in the First Commandment, beside what is revealed in the one word that is Jesus Christ, revealed and attested in the confession that Jesus is Lord; something "beside" that might and could and in his situation *did* become "besides" and "over against" me.[4]

The Prologue has a third role to play that is not to be overlooked. One of the primary dangers perceived in monotheistic religions—that is, systems that both deny the existence of other gods and require the worship of the one and only God—is that such exclusivism, allowing no alternative worldviews or forms of deity, breeds violence against those who do not buy into the system. Although I am writing in part against a reduction of the meaning and claim of the First Commandment to a rationalistic monotheism, such a danger is real and happens.[5] Scripture's own injunctions to destroy those who worship in a different way make us sharply aware of that.[6] In the Commandments one finds an implicit critique of such a way of responding. Over and against the impulse to destroy the other who does not worship the God you have is the ground that evokes the claim that the God you have is the only God you may have. That is what we hear in the divine self-assertion of the Prologue, the liberating grace of God that is set against all penultimate oppressive polities and has made covenant on the basis of the self-giving and liberating tender mercies. That is how the Commandments characterize and identify the God whose claims are indeed fully exclusive and permit no "and." One cannot talk generally about monotheism and its dangers and deal adequately with the God who meets freed slaves on Sinai and makes covenant and meets us in the face of Jesus Christ. There is a self-critique within the story itself.

There is also a complementary critique implicit in the second table of the Decalogue in its description of a way that one lives with "your neighbor," a moral and theological category—neighbor—that first comes into formal recognition in the Ten Commandments. Restrictive notions of the "neighbor" are called into question within the whole of Scripture. Thus within the Levitical code, the love of neighbor is extended explicitly to include the stranger or resident alien who is in the community (Lev 19:33-34). Jesus' parable of the Good Samaritan is as crucial for its recognition that the identity of your neighbor is not closed and is astonishingly open as it is for its teaching about modes of behavior toward the neighbor. The issue of the parable as raised by the questioner is precisely "Who is my neighbor?"[7] Jesus does not answer by a definition of the neighbor. He tells a story, even as the Prologue to the Commandments tells a story.

So it is that the community keeps learning how this God who demands is the God who frees and how the neighbor is to be found in strange and unexpected places. The Prologue and the second table of the Commandments frame the First Commandment so as to counter and resist the violence that may be read into it by monotheistic abstractions and by the practices of those who worship this Lord.

4

Translating Politically

So now we are already in the middle of the First Commandment, because you cannot talk about the Prologue without finishing the sentence where it ends, which is in the First Commandment, and you cannot talk about the First Commandment without knowing where it is coming from, which is the Prologue. Maybe somebody else can talk about it without talking about the Prologue, but not "you." So we are in the middle of the First Commandment, in the middle *and the end*. Because we do not know whether to translate the end of the commandment as "before me," "beside me," "besides me," or "over against me," we have to take them all. And all of them are caught up in Barth's "and"—"God and . . ." "revelation and . . ." For "you" there are no "ands"—there is only "the LORD your

God." The radical character of this demand is evident in the language used elsewhere to speak of the same commitment indicated in the Prologue and the First Commandment. We hear repeatedly the injunction to "follow" the Lord[1] and/or not to "follow" or "go after" other gods.[2] This is the language of discipleship, which begins not at Jesus' feet but in the First Commandment.

While we are in the translation issues and their significance for what it means to have a God, we need to attend to a feature of the text that is not a translation issue but often gets little attention beyond translation. "Before me or beside me or wherever, you shall have no other *gods.*" Not "other *god*" but other gods. We are regularly inclined to deal with this religiously and not theologically, reducing the issue to a history of religions question about whether Israel was monotheistic or polytheistic or something else. That is to abstract the Commandment from the story, which is not about religious alternatives, world constructs, and the like. It is about whom you trust and to whom you bow down, and who gets your praise. But even if talking about

polytheism versus monotheism takes us
away from the issue, the Commandment
does nevertheless speak about other *gods*.
The issue is not simply replacing the God
you have with another one but being
attracted by and succumbing to *multiple*
claims on your obedience.

One may say, and many do, that
monotheism is self-determining; the
nature of deity implies there can be only
one. That seems not to have been the case
with ancient Israel, however, and there is
no reason to assume that having only one
God is the only option so that the only
question would be which god are you
going to have as "your God." To make
such a monistic assumption is to move
from hierarchy (ultimate and penultimate
loyalties) to abstraction (deity=singular-
ity). The first tendency assumes the possibility of "God and . . ." The second lets
philosophical assumption—deity is one—
obscure the presence of all sorts of other
gods making their claims on our lives.
Either way risks turning discipleship into
intellectual choice, while in our lives
other gods are what we have. Beware of
thinking that being modern means being
educated into monotheism.

The monotheistic assumption leads us to view the many scriptural words and texts about conflicts between the Lord and the other gods as mythical remnants of no direct pertinence to a modern monotheistic world.[3] We either dismiss such accounts as vestiges of another time, a premodern, prerational time when polytheism was a live option, or we regard the battle as finally won and so no longer relevant to us because we know there is only one God. We would do well to discern in this dimension of Scripture some indication of the reality of other powers at work in the world whose ultimate conquest by the Lord of history is sure but whose power to entice and appeal, to exercise control over our lives, and thus to affect and effect history in other ways than those intended by the Lord your God is real and constantly present. They are to be *resisted* by human beings who are under the claim of the Prologue—"I am the LORD your God, who brought you out"—and the demand of the First Commandment "You shall have no other gods beside me." They are to be *fought* by the one whose self-revelation is in the conflict against the worldly

powers who enslave and claim to be the
lords of history, the pharaohs who dominate the world stage at every time, and
the gods they either claim to be or "follow after."

5

The Economic God

To stress the plurality of the gods who entice and allure us as much as they did the people of Israel is not, however, to lose the crucial issue in a vague generality of impulses and attractions. Whether with reference to the biblical story or more broadly to the picture that unfolds out of it in human history, the other gods have been dominated by two: Economy and Political Order (though we give them other names in the Bible and elsewhere), that is, the production and distribution, and consumption of things, of wealth, and the polity or government, the governing powers and authorities. The first of these is regularly identified in the Old Testament and in the New Testament. The other one is also clearly there if in more subtle but no less consequential ways.

The first, of course, is Baal. He is not really a problem if we can keep him confined to his good Canaanite name. Jesus gave this god an Aramaic name, Mammon, and the translations have varied in their history between leaving the Aramaic word alone or translating it "wealth" (Matt 6:24; Luke 16:13 [cf. vv. 14-15]). There are obvious reasons for the latter move, but there are also important reasons why the church kept the Aramaic word in the Gospels; it is a personification, which makes it difficult to mistake the issue of *other gods.* Not only do Jesus' introductory words about not serving two masters indicate the issue is the god you have versus the god you want, but his use of "Mammon" makes it clear that this is one of the *other gods.* Later tradition reinforced that as, in the Middle Ages, Mammon was seen as the devil of covetousness. And the poet Coleridge warned about the danger of "mammonolatry."[1] Furthermore, while the etymology is not altogether certain, it is likely that the name is derived from the word *'āman,* "that in which one trusts." I do not know how good Jesus was at etymologies, but he knew what the First Commandment was all about.

These Canaanite and Aramaic names—Baal and Mammon—let us know that it is the First Commandment that is at stake. Those strange and distant names, however, cannot shield us from the lure of this god, Wealth. It is not just wealth, of course; it is the system of productivity and distribution that creates the wealth and the consumption that sees I get mine. It is Gomer's lovers, most prominently Baal, who "give me my bread and my water, my wool and my flax, my oil and my drink" (Hos 2:5; cf. vv. 13, 16–17). This god goes by other names as well. In Jeremiah she is the Queen of Heaven. When Jeremiah denounces the exiles in Egypt for making offerings to "other gods," the people adamantly refuse to stop, because when they made those offerings in the past, they "used to have plenty of food, and prospered, and saw no misfortune" (Jer 44:17).

Critical to the story of Jeremiah and the exiles is the realization that we are not talking here only about individualized acquisitive instincts or habits but about communal devotion to the gods of productivity and systemic efforts to elicit provision and wealth from them. That is why Mammon is not simply an abstraction—wealth—or a personal god. Mammon is what it takes to make the system more productive and provide more possibility for consumption. Most of the worship of other gods that goes on in the Scriptures is a communal enterprise. It is systemic because it has to do with the systems of making and spending, of getting and having. One of the things you can do with the God you have is believe that you can have more with another god. The god is the symbol, often highly visible, of the productivity and consumption that has erected it.

The translation possibilities and uncertainties, therefore, highlight the problem. It is not simply other gods "besides me." It is also the matter of placing another god alongside/beside "me" or "before"—that is, in front of me, "God and . . ." I claim obedience to the Lord, but alongside that I want to get mine. My anxieties about that reveal where I really put my trust, and who or what I think really sustains my life. When Jesus takes up this issue, he argues the impossibility of serving two masters. We need to be careful not to focus primarily on the logical point he argues—you will love one and hate the other—but on where he ends up. It may in fact be possible to serve two masters and split one's loyalties—until they come in conflict with each other. The God who frees slaves oppressed by the civil powers who seek to extract more wealth out of those who serve them and at the cheapest cost possible, who squeeze the budget, whether by cutting out the straw or cutting back the value of food stamps, is always opposed to and over against Mammon when the wealth and consumer system is the primary thing that commands our attention. So ultimately Jesus is correct, not so much in behalf of an abstract or logical principle about whether it is possible to serve two masters but whether it is possible to serve *these* two masters.

Other gods, in principle and practice, can be multiple, innumerable, maybe a pantheon of 400, as in the polytheistic systems of some of the ancient Near Eastern powers, but the story of Israel and the church is not that story. It knows that the other gods who attract our obedience are limited, and that from the first "golden" calf—which the community of faith built out of their plundered wealth because they did not trust the God who had redeemed them to care for them and worried about their ability to make it—until the present, one of those gods to whom the community of faith and its members regularly turn is the only one Jesus ever talked about—the system of wealth, getting and spending, having and holding.

The radical character of Jesus' instruction on this matter must not be overlooked. There is a tension that cannot be easily resolved but is always before us. It is perhaps seen most clearly in the wisdom traditions. In Sirach and the Psalms, for example, the goods we possess are a divine provision, a gift of God:

> Likewise all to whom God gives wealth and possessions and whom he enables to enjoy them, and to accept their lot and find enjoyment in their toil—this is the gift of God. (Sirach 5:19; cf. 6:2)

> Happy are those who fear the Lord...
> Wealth and riches are in their houses,
>   and their righteousness endures
>   forever. (Ps 112:1,3)

Ecclesiastes speaks of those to whom "God gives wealth and possessions" (Eccl. 5:19; 6:2).

Alongside this conviction, however, Sirach assumes what seems clearly to be implied also by Jesus' completely negative words about Mammon, to the effect that "in practice no property can be acquired except with some element of injustice":[2]

> A merchant can hardly keep from wrongdoing, nor is a tradesman innocent of sin. Many have committed sin for gain, and those who seek to get rich will avert their eyes. As a stake is driven firmly into a fissure between stones, so sin is wedged in between selling and buying. (Sirach 26:29–27:2)

Psalm 52:7 makes this same point in language that unmistakably sets the issue as one that has to do directly with obedience to the First Commandment:

> See the one who would
> *not take refuge in God,*
> But *trusted in abundant riches,*
> *And sought refuge in wealth.*

And in the last of Job's speeches, his long protestation of innocence in chapter 31, one of the tests of his righteousness is:

> If I have made gold my trust,
> Or called fine gold my confidence . . .
> (Job 31:24)

In the case of Jesus' radical instruction, however, there seems to be no tension, only the assumption that property and wealth are another god, an alternative master in whom one is always at risk of putting one's trust and finding a place of ultimate refuge.

6

The Political Order as Other God

Various texts of Scripture illustrate and illumine the undoing of the First Commandment in the actions of the *political order* and responses to it. One may cite the story of the ark and the destruction of the Philistine god Dagon in the Philistine sanctuary as a narrative account of the battle of the gods (1 Sam 5:1-5). The Philistines, victorious in the battle of Ebenezer/Aphek, capture the Ark of the Covenant, the earthly throne of the Lord of Israel, and take it to the house or temple of Dagon in the Philistine city of Ashdod. There they place it alongside the statue of the Philistine god Dagon. In the morning they find the statue has fallen on its face before the Ark. Replaced by the priests, the statue is found the second

morning having fallen over again, but
this time with its head and hands cut off.
No deity alongside or in hostile confrontation with this God! If it is alongside,
it will be knocked down. If it is in hostile
confrontation, it will have its hands and
head cut off. The only way for any other
being—divine or human—to come before
this deity is prostrate in worship. The presumption of the power of other gods is
brought to naught as the "other god" is
discovered first in prostration and worship before the Lord of Israel and then
with its presumed divine power destroyed.

What is particularly interesting about
this story is that, in this instance, the
meaning of the First Commandment is
dramatized and worked out not among
the Israelites, but among the Philistines.
One begins to see the address of the Commandment breaking out of the covenant
community, out of a particular linguistic,
cultural community—to use the language
of George Lindbeck[1]—to make an increas-
ingly universal claim. In this context,
two things are to be remembered. First, in
the prophecy of Amos, the Lord says,
"Did I not also bring up the Philistines
from Caphtor . . . ?" (Amos 9:7) thereby

claiming an *exodus* relation to the *Philistines* also! Second, the Psalms regularly call for the nations of the earth to bow down and praise the Lord of Israel. The "you" of the First Commandment begins to be stretched. The claim of the commandment on others is learned from the story, however, not from natural law or rational deduction.

The presumption of power on the part of the political order in denial of the claim of the First Commandment occurs also in the show trial and subsequent execution of Naboth because King Ahab covets his vegetable garden and is told by his wife, Jezebel, that he is ruler and in charge and so can do what he wishes, even if it means lying, stealing, and murder, as it does in this case (1 Kings 21). The story is a demonstration of political hubris that presumes a freedom from the constraints of the second table of the Commandments. In doing so, the king thus implicitly rejects the claims of the first table that are the grounds for the second.

The best example may be a subtler one. It is the encounter between the chief priest at Bethel and the prophet Amos, who has been sent by the Lord from Judah in the

south to prophesy in the Northern Kingdom, Israel. When they meet, the priest
tells Amos to leave town. His framing of
the demand is what is revealing. Here are
his words, first to the king, then to Amos:

> Then Amaziah, the priest of Bethel,
> sent to King Jeroboam of Israel, say-
> ing, "Amos has conspired against you
> in the very center of the house of
> Israel; the land is not able to bear all
> his words. For thus Amos has said:
>> 'Jeroboam shall die by the sword,
>>> and Israel must go into exile
>>> away from his land.'"
>
> And Amaziah said to Amos, "O
> seer, go, flee away to the land of
> Judah, earn your bread there, and
> prophesy there; but never again
> prophesy at Bethel, for it is the king's
> sanctuary, and it is a temple of the
> kingdom."
>
> Then Amos answered Amaziah, "I
> am no prophet, nor a prophet's son;
> but I am a herdsman, and a dresser of
> sycamore trees, and the LORD took me
> from following the flock, and the LORD
> said to me, 'Go, prophesy to my peo-
> ple Israel.'" (Amos 7:10-14)

Amos's choice of words is significant. "Amos has conspired against you [the king] in the very center of the house of Israel." The priest's concern is legitimate because Amos did indeed say that Jeroboam would die by the sword. But he did not say it quite that way, and the difference is significant (see below). First, the location of the threat is described as "the house of Israel," an accurate phrase, seemingly of no consequence in this context. That is precisely the point, however. The significance of Israel's identity as uncovered in the First Commandment and the Prologue has disappeared from the political scene to be replaced with an ethnic identification that has forgotten from whence Israel came. When Amos responds to the priest of Bethel, the national shrine of the Northern Kingdom, he says that the Lord took him from following the flock and said, "Go prophesy to *my people* Israel. Not *"the house of* Israel,*"* but *"my people* Israel." Two apparently innocuous differences conceal crucial and totally different perspectives: (1) the political entity is understood by the political power as just that, the state, and thus under the ruler's control and subject to his will; and (2) the religious leadership of the community, the priest anointed by the Lord, is fully complicit in this understanding. The representative of the Lord to the people perceives them only as the house of Israel. Thus Amos's response about his assignment, which recharacterizes the polis as "my people Israel," is an invocation of the claim of the First Commandment (including the Prologue) against its disappearance in the rhetoric of the religious and theological leadership.

Second, the priestly servant of the state has converted the prophet's regular "Thus says the LORD," into "Thus Amos has said," and the prophetic word, "*I (the LORD)* will rise against the house of Jeroboam with the sword" (7:9) has been converted into "Jeroboam shall die by the sword."[2] In other words, the religious spokesman as political spokesman completely detheologizes the prophetic message, so that the only authority on the scene, actual or implicit—the only authority on the scene to whom the chief priest is accountable—is the king, the leader of the political order.[3]

Lest one think the point too subtle to be firm, the further words of Amaziah the priest of Bethel, this time directly to Amos, make it more blatant. Like the sheriff in an old western movie, he tells Amos to get out of town, to go home to Judah and do his prophesying there, and never prophesy again in Bethel, "because it is"—not the house of the Lord and/or the temple of the Lord but—"*the king's sanctuary* and the *temple of the kingdom*." The church is coterminus with the East Wing of the White House, in effect. Amos may not preach in the national church any longer because it is now both royal chapel and national cathedral. The political authority has taken over the religious center and claimed it for its own. It is doubly a political center and not a place whose identity is defined by the Lord whose worship is its center. The political lord is the center of meaning and value in this sanctuary, the one who gives it identity, not "the LORD your God, who brought you out of the land of Egypt, out of the house of slavery."

While resisting finding in the *political order* or the *state* and its powers other gods that may draw us away from the God who has freed us in grace and mercy, we nevertheless must also ask what place does the polis, with its power and its authority, have. Like the economy, the political order is one of the frameworks for human flourishing without which we descend into communal and moral chaos. Jesus affirms the separation of that earthly power from the worship of God in his response to those who would test him about paying taxes—an excellent example then and now for the possibility of both political order and economy becoming "other gods" (Matt. 22:17; Mark 12:14; Luke 20:22). While Jesus' answer was a succinct and unelaborated distinction between all earthly civil power and the God you have, it was also an acknowledgment of the place of such civil power. For the political order as much as for the economy, one cannot give them up even as one cannot have them as gods. If the economy can enhance human flourishing without becoming a god—by trusting that what you have comes from the God you have and being willing to let one's focus be upon the *God* you have more than *what* you have—then the political order can enhance human community and the common good by being the context of our life with the neighbor as much as it is a potential threat to our proper life with God. Indeed, without a polity of some sort, a large common good with the neighbor is well nigh impossible either to achieve or to discover.

When the apostle Paul takes up the Commandments in Romans 13:8-10, he refers to most of the commandments of the *second* table of the Decalogue as subsumed under or manifestations of the love of neighbor. But Romans 13, of course, is Paul's famous discussion of the place of the governing authorities and Christian responsibility before the political authorities and the powers that be. He is discussing the authorities, to whom one pays taxes as appropriate and to whom one gives honor as appropriate, which is probably why he moves toward the second table of the Decalogue.[4] The reference to "honor" is a clue that he is now operating out of the Fifth Commandment about honoring parents, which, from at least the time of Deuteronomy to the present, has been understood as also providing direction to the covenantal community about how individual members are to live in relation to the authorities and powers of the community: respect to those to whom respect is due and honor to whom honor is due.[5] The powers that be properly receive honor and respect, via the injunction of the Fifth Commandment to honor parents and, by implication and analogy, all other properly constituted authorities and leaders. But *that* is where the authorities come into the moral framework provided by the Commandments, not in relation to the First Commandment. The distinction is critical for maintaining the proper honor and respect that allow the community to function in good health and to insure that the human powers that be do not become the other gods in whom we place all our trust and to whom our loyalty becomes more important than our obedience to God.

For this reason, I find myself thinking more and more of the Commandments as having to do with *obedience* rather than *loyalty*. Loyalty, in the sense of allegiance to the government of one's country, is appropriate to being a citizen and to the protection and flourishing of the polis, the civic and political order. Obedience belongs to God. There is a place for *civil* disobedience in the context of obedience to the only God you have. There is no place for the other gods, even if, indeed especially when, they look like the leaders of the polis, the politicians, the powers that be. It is important, therefore, to distinguish loyalty from discipleship, a mode of living that has its origins, as noted above, precisely in the claim of the First Commandment. The God you have is the one you shall follow after. You shall have no other gods to follow after.

When it confessed, "Jesus is Lord," the Christian church either broke utterly its fundamental First Commandment obligation or it found its true Lord. It was, of course, this confession that was then set against the temptation to place the political power as the center of meaning and value, the ultimate object of the community's allegiance—the worship of the emperor. Not Augustus but Jesus is Lord. 1 Peter 2:17 makes it clear how the Christian community continued to live by the First Commandment:

> Honor everyone. Love the family of believers. Fear God. Honor the emperor.

Note the difference between what you do with God you have and what you do with the emperor. God is to be feared and worshiped. The emperor is to be treated like everyone else—with honor.

It is important to recognize, however, that even in this sphere the *imitation of Christ* is still operative. The claim that Jesus is Lord is the revelation of God in the light of the resurrection. It is not a claim that Jesus himself makes. On the contrary, when the tempter bids Jesus fall down and worship him, Jesus cites the Deuteronomic form of the First Commandment: "Worship the Lord your God and serve only him" (Matt 4:10).

Thus I find myself perplexed that those of us for whom the First Commandment is indeed not simply "a" political axiom but "the" political axiom often justify our criticism of the government and of its leaders and their actions primarily on the grounds of a proper understanding of patriotism and the rights of free speech, which include dissent. That, however, is not where Christians come from. It is the First Commandment, not the First Amendment that frees us for any and all criticism of the political order and of the politicians. The God you have is the only God you have, and thus you are free from all restraints against the critique of lesser powers in this world. Discipleship and obedience are rendered to the Lord your God. Various loyalties, including loyalty to one's land and country compete for our sincere response. Such loyalties are real—they can be seen and felt—and they matter. But they are penultimate. You can have only one God and Lord.

7

The Positive Meanings of
the First Commandment

The interpretation of the First Commandment to this point has focused primarily on its *prohibitive* dimensions with some suggestions in the previous chapter of a positive force that is implicit in the negative or explicit in the critical text. John Calvin's hermeneutic of the Commandments—which insists that every negative command, every prohibition, has its positive corollary and that every positive command implies negative actions as well—is found in Scripture itself. So, for example, within the positive Sabbath commandment there is a negative form as well: "You shall not do any work." And the Fifth Commandment has its negative formulation in the Book of the Covenant: "Whoever strikes father or mother shall be put to death" (Exod 21:15).

Positive instruction, teaching about what to do as well as what not to do is especially prominent in the case of the First Commandment. Its positive corollary is found especially in two places. One of these is Deuteronomy's abstraction from the Commandments of their essence in the Shema, the Great Commandment: "Hear, O Israel, the LORD is our God, the LORD alone [or "the LORD is one"]; so you shall love the LORD your God with all your heart and with all your soul and with all your might" (Deut. 6:4-5). The positive form of the First Commandment is as important for directing our way of living and being, thinking and acting, as is the negative. This positive articulation, however, forces us to think more expansively than the negative does. The negative gives us a pointed prohibition that is fundamental to Christian identity and to our capacity to live as Christians in a world where the political powers and the economy dominate. The positive completely fills our lives with its injunction to love the Lord your God with all your heart and all your soul and all that you are and have.

I will not go into an extended elaboration of the Shema, but I do want to make an observation relative to the preceding discussion about the other gods. Prohibition of the worship of the god of wealth-economy-production-consumption and the god of country-state-polis has its positive formulation in the Shema in three ways:

1. The love of God is that combination of action and feeling, of obedience and devotion, that is not to be directed toward any other object except the neighbor. Thus, it is as one devotes oneself to the Lord that all other claims, that is, other gods, are squeezed out of the system. They *have no place*, according to the prohibition, so you cannot have any other gods; they *lose their place* as you find yourself absorbed in the love of God. Clearly, there are theological and ethical, along with other kinds of issues that arise in regard to the various relationships that place claims on us. But the love of the Lord your God is the vehicle—involving act and affect—that provides the means

for sorting out these other claims and not allowing them to take over.

2. Even the love of neighbor is secondary in a sense, not only as the *second* table, the *second* great commandment, but also in that this command does not carry the amplifying characterization present in the primary commandment: "with all your heart, with all your soul, and with all your might."

3. From earliest times, the tradition has widely understood the love of the Lord "with all your might" as not only handing over your affections, your will, your obedience, but also handing over your wealth and property and possessions, even to the point of impoverishment, according to Calvin. What that actually involves is a complex matter that each disciple has to work out. Because the claim itself is a rejection of the focus on wealth and property, one's possessions are always for the sake of relinquishment. It is precisely when possession is for its own sake or even for *our* own sake that the single devotion breaks down and Mammon appears on the scene.

4. "With all your heart and with all your soul and with all your might" reinforces the totality of this commitment. In that sense it is the fullness of being, act, and affect—the way we are, what we do, and how we feel.[1]

That totality of commitment has, in fact, been witnessed again and again, although perhaps no more starkly than in the death of Rabbi Akiva in the second century of the Common Era, a story that has become an indelible part of Jewish tradition.

During the time of Hadrian—when relations between the Jewish community and the Roman authorities disintegrated and the Romans destroyed the Jewish resistance, killed thousands of Jews, forbade the few remaining Jews to practice their religion, and finally in 134 CE forbade even the study of the Torah—the great rabbi and leader of the Jewish community, Akiba, who had continued to teach the Torah against the Roman decree, was imprisoned and brought to trial. Here is how biographer Louis Finkelstein describes Akiba's end and concludes his biography of this great Jewish leader:

Akiba was found guilty and condemned to death. Still attended by his faithful Joshua, he retained his courage and his strength of mind until the very end. The popular story tells that the Romans killed him by tearing his flesh from his living body. As he lay in unspeakable agony, he suddenly noticed the first streaks of dawn breaking over the eastern hills. It was the hour when the Law requires each Jew to pronounce the *Shema*. Oblivious to his surroundings, Akiba intoned in a loud, steady voice, the forbidden words of his faith, "Hear, O Israel, the Lord is our God, the Lord is One. And thou shalt love the Lord thy God with all thine heart, and with all thy soul, and with all thy might."

Rufus, the Roman general, who superintended the horrible execution, cried out: "Are you a wizard or are you utterly insensible to pain?"

"I am neither," replied the martyr, "but all my life I have been waiting for the moment when I might truly fulfill this commandment. I have always loved the Lord with all my might, and with all my heart; now I know that I

love him with all my life." And repeat-
ing the verse again, he died as he
reached the words, "The Lord is one."[2]

Typical of other positive forms of the
First Commandment, particularly in
Deuteronomy, is the following extensive
elaboration of the First Commandment in
positive terms. It is often overlooked but
provides large clues to what is at stake:

> The Lord your God you shall follow,
> him alone you shall fear, his command-
> ments you shall keep, his voice you
> shall obey, him you shall serve, and to
> him you shall hold fast. (Deut 13:4)

The opening clause, I have already
suggested, is the positive form of the
prohibition of the First Commandment.
The clauses that follow direct us to other
aspects of loving the Lord your God,
providing at least four responses to the
question: What do you do with the God
you have? They are: trust, reverence,
conscience, and praise.

1. The final and climactic command of
the verse is "to him you shall hold fast [or

"cleave"]." Like skin to bone, like scales of a fish, like a tongue to the roof of the mouth, it describes a form of loyalty that is intended. Once again, however, loyalty does not adequately say what is really meant here. The loyalty of the First Commandment is *trust*, and there is much more there than is involved in loyalty. The latter, which includes devotion, a giving of oneself in behalf of the other, does not say as clearly that the giving involves the possibility of living by risk and not worrying about it, living toward promise and knowing that the promise, however far off, is good, a total giving of oneself that is ultimately in behalf of oneself.[3]

We often miss the extent to which trust in the Lord, treating the promises of God as reliable, is a full devotion that is also fully *reciprocated*. The love of God manifest in such total clinging and holding fast is response to a love that we have received, a love that is a prior reality, a presupposition of our trust in God. But it is also a continuing reality, as when one clings to a parent in utter dependence in the implicit but real confidence that such trust is founded on a promised security. We love because we have first been loved, the meaning of the Prologue again. The trust that is commanded in the First Commandment is our way through the wilderness, for it is found precisely as one sets the Lord as the only reliable reference point for all of our life.

"A mighty fortress is our God." The psalms regularly speak of trust in the Lord as manifest in finding your only secure refuge in the God you have.[4] So in Psalm 62 the First Commandment becomes a part of the life of devotion and the only hope in a world whose precariousness is definitional but not foundational:

> For God alone my soul waits in
>   silence;
> From him comes my salvation.
> He alone is my rock and my salvation,
>   My fortress; I shall never be
>   shaken. (Ps 62:1–2)

Again and again, Psalm 62 repeats this embedded form of the First Commandment and then turns to the congregation and says this is what it means for you:

> Trust in him at all times, O people;
>   Pour out your heart before him;
> God is a refuge for us. (Ps 62:8)

More than once, the Psalms set this refuge and trust in the Lord over against the human tendency to trust in princes, rulers, and the great ones of the earth, indeed in any mortal human being (Ps 118:8–9; 146:3–4).

The political meaning of this theme is self-evident but not confined to political activities alone. On the one hand it means that risk is possible in the face of the power—actual and potential—of the political orders and the lure of the economy. Both spheres are places for living and for moral reflection and action, but they are not the objects of our trust. So because our refuge is elsewhere, we do not have to be afraid. Precisely at that point the commandment comes to us as gospel, and we hear its evangelical force. On the other hand, when we are undone and unable to overcome the powers that afflict our lives, the cry to God is the act of deepest trust. In the midst of that paradigmatic cry for help, Psalm 22, we hear the psalmist remember the story of his fathers and mothers and the parallelism of the sentences is inescapable:

In you our ancestors *trusted;*
> They *trusted,* and you delivered
> them.
To you they *cried,* and were saved;
> In you they t*rusted,* and were not
> put to shame. (Ps 22:4–5)

So the prayer to the Lord your God is one of the most explicit acts of obedience to the First Commandment. It is what you do with the God you have that separates this one from all the other possibilities, from all other attractions and potential claims on your devotion.

2. Deuteronomy 13:4 further adds to its interpretation of the First Commandment, "He is the one you shall fear." That is, under the First Commandment life is lived in the *deepest reverence and awe* before the Holy and Wholly Other, whose name for us is "the LORD your God." Of course, with such language as "fearing God," we are talking about worship and obedience, but it is in the language of fear and awe that we encounter something of the depth of the affective dimension of our worship of God. Such reverence is manifest in many ways, some more action—bowing of

head and knee, guarding the name in speech—others more emotion—tears, joy, awe, and even fear and shame. Such fear of God is experienced and manifest in the context of formal worship and holy place; it is also experienced, manifest, and nurtured in practices of devotion. Indeed, the devotional life—public and private, however it is practiced—is the development of a proper fear of the Lord, and so a keeping and obeying of the First Commandment.

If there is a reciprocality in the experience of obedience as trust, found in being able to count upon the one who has loved and promised, there is a different kind of outflow from the experience of reverence and awe before the Lord your God. It is the possibility that in such a way before God, we learn reverence not only as commandment but also as virtue, not only as a form of obedience toward God but also as a way with our neighbor. Again the political dimension of this way of feeling and being is evident and potent. Reverence means that one can no more treat the world and its populace casually and without respect than one can the Lord your God. Plato tells of Protagoras inventing a myth of Zeus as follows:

Whenever they [that is, early human beings] gathered into groups, they would do wrong to each other, because they did not yet have the knowledge of how to form society. As a result they would scatter again and perish. And so Zeus, fearing that our whole species would be wiped out, sent Hermes to bring Reverence and Justice to human beings, in order that these two would adorn society and bind people together in friendship.[5]

In his small book on reverence, Paul Woodruff summarizes this as follows:

Protagoras invented a myth in which the highest god gave reverence and justice to human beings as means for the survival of society. Reverence and justice supplement an earlier gift of fire and technology, which Prometheus stole for us from the gods, hoping that they would keep our species alive. But Zeus saw that technology alone, without virtue, is no defense against mutual destruction.[6]

Neither Protagoras nor Plato, much less Paul Woodruff, had in mind the Commandments, but it is there that the community of faith learns the virtues of reverence (the first table) and justice (the second table). But Plato and Protagoras do, by inference, remind us that the first table, which has to do with our worship of the only God we have, also lays the foundation for the second table. As we have noted above, that connection is explicit in regard to the experience of *honor and reverence*; the Fifth Commandment instructs us to give to parents and, by implication, other authorities, the reverence and respect that are like what we give to the Lord. It does not stop there, however, for once reverence becomes a mode of feeling and being and acting, its range is comprehensive. If, as Woodruff rightly suggests, the basic components of reverence are awe, respect, and shame, then reverence makes it impossible, even in the midst of war, to say, in contempt of others and without shame before God: "We wanted to kill them all but some got away." Reverence makes it impossible to count only the dead and wounded of your society and not those of your enemy.

3. "His commandments you shall keep; his voice you shall obey." It is here in this elaboration of the First Commandment that one encounters the *conscience.* The idiom that is so familiar to us, "the voice of conscience," is apt in this instance. For it is precisely the question, To whom do you listen? that is at stake in the First Commandment and makes it politically axiomatic. The voice of conscience is the issue of who it is one obeys. The substance of that obedience is always given in the Commandments, the First Commandment being both part of the whole and the exhaustion of the whole. For many, the conscience is some sort of internal moral impulse. I would rather stay with Deuteronomy and the voice. The voice of the conscience is the Lord of the conscience, and the Lord of the conscience is the only God you have. So listen to "his voice" only. Following one's conscience is discipleship if it is life lived by the Commandments.

As the Westminster Confession of Faith takes up the matter of conscience, there are three aspects of its treatment that belong to our reflection on the First Commandment.[7] First, the subject of conscience appears in the Confession immediately following its discussion of the law as embodied in the Commandments, securing the connection between the Commandments and the voice of conscience. Here, therefore, is a confessional reflection of the Deuteronomic joining of "his commandments you shall keep" and "his voice you shall obey." Second, it understands conscience in the context of Christian liberty. To talk about the conscience in the context of Christian faith and the Commandments is to talk about both freedom and restraint and about how they are embodied and held in tension in the meaning of conscience. Thus we encounter a confessional echo of the joining of Prologue and First Commandment, the tension between being free and being under command. Third, it is necessary at the conclusion of this section of the Confession to provide a long paragraph explaining that there is no contradiction between "the power which God has ordained"—that is, the polis, the political power—and "the liberty which Christ has purchased." Christian freedom, therefore, is not to be regarded as a license for civil disobedience and rebellion against the political authorities. How one deals with this confessional safeguard and the tension that it lifts up is not my concern here. The point I am making is that the tension is there, that the political implication of the issue of conscience, of "his voice you shall obey," is immediately present and unavoidable.

4. Finally, we come to the "*end*" of the First Commandment—the end in a double sense. One is provided by the familiar first question of the Westminster Shorter Catechism: "What is man's chief end?" What is the main purpose of human existence? The answer is succinct and to the point: "to glorify God and enjoy him forever." The Catechism begins with the First Commandment and defines it in terms of our chief purpose, our primary reason for being in this world: *the praise of God.* The letter to the Ephesians says the same thing in christological fashion:

> In Christ we have also obtained an inheritance, having been destined according to the purpose of him who accomplishes all things according to his counsel and will, so that we, who were the first to set our hope on

Christ, might live for the praise of his glory. (Eph 1:11-12)

The authors of the Westminster Confession would also have understood the correlation of an inherent or created dimension of our humanity and the divine instruction in the First Commandment. By having been created human and by keeping the First Commandment, we find ourselves destined to be creatures of praise. Like crying out in prayer, the songs of praise are a powerful answer to the question of what we do with the God we have. We sing the praises of the Lord our God. That is our reason for being, that is our most articulate act, that is our fullest emotion. In so doing, we find ourselves in the holy place making the largest of claims about all other places, both the market and the political order. We do not sing their praises; we do not set our trust there. All our praise finally subverts any possibility that we can have another God. The community that sings the praises of God can hardly give its ultimate allegiance to any human claim for power over us. We have entered another service. We have learned to say Amen.

And so the Psalter, which is the book of Scripture that gives us the voice of praise to respond to the voice we obey, becomes for the church a kind of political manual. In what are surely the most conspicuously and comprehensively political documents in all of Scripture, the Psalter culminates in an extravagant, all-encompassing concert of praise in its final psalms, calling earth and heaven, all their creatures and all their peoples to the praise of God.[8]

The First Commandment thus defines who we are and what we are about in this world. It is not subject to malleability or occasional departures. If the Lord of Israel is the one who made us and the world of which we are a part; if the Lord of Israel is the only one who can take away our fear and save us in our trouble, if the Lord of Israel has alone brought us to this place and is alone our hope for the future, then all our trust and all our obedience and all our adoration are placed there and nowhere else. That, I think, is a piece of good news that serves to relativize all the other demands and claims on our life. But if all that is really true, it is a reality that we cannot walk in and out of, looking for some other cosmic system, some other ground on which to stand, some other deliverer. For one thing, there isn't any; and for the other, our very identity is established by the exclusive worship of this God who has loved us and redeemed us. You cannot walk two ways at the same time. You cannot live in two different worlds at the same time. The God who speaks to us in Scripture is not friendly except to human beings. The stories of the Lord's war against the other gods (e.g., cutting off the hands and head of Dagon of the Philistines) is a narrative way of telling us that there are all sorts of possibilities out there to lure our worship and obedience, but the maker of heaven and earth is a jealous God and will have none of it. One of the chief ways in which we domesticate God is to assume the kind of friendliness, selflessness, and tolerance on the part of God that we hope is present in each of us. The jealousy and wrath of God are reminders that God is not meant to be likable but to be God. The joy and praise we render is to the God who has redeemed us and taken away our fears so that we can live in this world.

The celebration is over the fact that the power undergirding everything is loving and on our side. The cross, however, tells us this is a painful love, and the First Commandment tells us it cannot be played with or taken for granted. Another way of putting it is that we are in this Christian skin, and we cannot get out of it without killing ourselves.

8

The First Commandment and the First Table

I have suggested that when speaking about the First Commandment one inevitably has to deal with the first table of the Decalogue and not simply the first prohibition after the Prologue. There are various reasons why that is so, some of which have to do with grammar, syntax, word association, and the like. I am interested at this point, however, in the *substantive* ways in which the other commandments of the first table of the Decalogue represent the fullness of what is intended in the First Commandment. I do not think one can fully comprehend what the First Commandment is about if these inherent connections are ignored.

To the extent that the commandments that follow the Prologue and the First

Commandment are a way of learning
what to do with the God you have, one
may set out their movement and inner
connections in the following succinct
way:

1. The First Commandment is a way of
requiring that you take the God you have
with *ultimate seriousness.* All of the
above is an effort to explicate the content
of both the ultimacy and the seriousness.

2. The Second Commandment, which
warns us against the attractiveness of the
things of this world as objects of worship
and indeed replacements or surrogates
for the only God you have, is a way of
requiring us *not to take anything else too
seriously,* especially the things we have
made that may be attractive and luring. I
have already talked about the lure of
wealth and power. Of course, eventually,
one would have to talk about the *images*
that most attract us and become substi-
tutes for the only God we have, specifically theological images. Learning to do
theology under the First Commandment
is a way of learning to be both *kataphatic*
and *apophatic* at the same time, that is,

learning to name God by saying who or what God is with the language and images available to us but also to name God by saying who or what God is not. At the same time that we construct our theological images, we also tear them down. Deuteronomy is suggestive at this point with its tension between the voice out of the fire but no form and its report of the people's encounter with the presence of God at Sinai in the paradox of "the mountain blazing with fire, darkness, cloud, and deep gloom" (Deut 4:11). Perhaps the only image of God that will ever hold together the *apophatic* and the *kataphatic* and is also untouchable and cannot be made, is fire. But then reverence is our way with others in no small measure because there is an image of the Lord that is accessible and worthy of our honor and respect and reverence, an image that points us to the Lord our God but is not the Lord our God. As one of my colleagues once put it, that image is made by God, walks on two feet, and sings the praises of its Creator.

3. If the First Commandment is instruction about taking the Lord your God with

ultimate seriousness and the Second Commandment about not taking anything else too seriously, the Third Commandment is instruction not to take the Lord your God, the only God you have, *too lightly*, not to go about as if the name of the Lord did not make any difference, as Paul Lehmann puts it.[1] *Kataphasis* and *apophasis*–saying something and saying nothing–have their interplay with the name of the Lord your God as well. For this reason, Jews and others will speak "the name" instead of speaking the name.[2] So we hear a command not to be casual when we use the name, that is, not to misuse the name by invoking it as the grounding of what we do and say when what we do and say is not serious. If God is to be taken with ultimate seriousness, then whatever is said in God's name is of ultimate seriousness and so cannot accompany lies, euphemisms, exaggerations, profanations, and political claims. There is scarcely a politician among us who is capable of invoking the name of God as if it made any difference other than the securing of political endorsement. So do not go about with all your "God bless Americas," as if the name of

God can be a tool for political manipulation rather than reverence and praise.

4. Fourth, then, the Sabbath Command, in some ways the hardest of all the commandments to keep, is there to help us *take God seriously and ourselves lightly.* Everything is let go so that with constant regularity our life is given over to the service of the only God, the one we have. In that process, we let go of self and all those things that have become our self-justification or our self-indulgence. The rabbis thought that the Sabbath provided a glimpse of the world to come. I think they were right and that we might be clearer about that if we knew how to keep the Sabbath holy and wholly.

Finally, it must be acknowledged that there are no principles here, only a divine command and a conversation about its axiomatic character and how it addresses the question, "What do you do with the God you have?" What remains is clear from the Scriptures. To learn further how it directs us, read the stories. They begin immediately after the Commandments and go to the end. In fact, they are still going on, and—whether they are about golden calves or American flags—they are political all the way.

Notes

Chapter 1

1. Karl Barth, "The First Commandment as an Axiom of Theology," in *The Way of Theology in Karl Barth: Essays and Comments*, ed. H. Martin Rumscheidt (Allison Park, Pa.: Pickwick Publications, 1986), 77. Barth's "No!" to natural theology was a resistance to any move to see in creation and the orders of nature a revelation of God that could stand alongside the revelation of God in the word that comes to us in Jesus Christ, the Scriptures, and the preaching of the gospel.

2. See, e.g., Paul Lehmann, *Ethics in a Christian Context* (New York: Harper and Row, 1963), 74–101; also Lehmann, *The Transfiguration of Politics: The Presence and Power of Jesus of Nazareth in and over Human Affairs* (New York: Harper and Row, 1975). Note the comment of Hans Frei: "[T]here is no such thing as a Christian theology which is not together with other things also a political theology" (cited by M. A. Higton, in "'A Carefully Circumscribed Progressive Politics': Hans Frei's Political Theology," *Modern Theology* 15 [1999]: 53).

3. The numeration followed here, typical of the Reformed tradition, distinguishes between the Prologue and the prohibition against having other

gods (the First Commandment) and between that prohibition and the commandment against making and worshipping images (the Second Commandment). At the same time, there are strong arguments for tying the Prologue to the prohibition of other gods, as in the Jewish tradition, as well as for seeing the prohibition of other gods and of images as being a single comprehensive command, as in the Lutheran tradition. In the pages that follow, "First Commandment" refers to the prohibition, "You shall have no other gods . . . ," but I will also try to show the interaction between that commandment and what precedes and follows it.

4. Barth, "The First Commandment as an Axiom of Theology," 62.

5. "The 'German Christians' were those among the Protestant churches under Hitler who were most keen to bring about a synthesis between Nazism and Christianity, identifying religious aims with national aims" (Eberhard Busch, *Karl Barth: His Life from Letters and Autobiographical Texts* [Philadelphia: Fortress Press, 1976], 224).

6. Arthur C. Cochrane, *The Church's Confession under Hitler* (Philadelphia: Westminster, 1962), 135.

7. "The 'Confessing Church' grew out of the 'Pastors' Emergency League' founded by Martin Niemöller in 1933, taking its name from the fact that it based its opposition to Hitler and the

'German Christians' on the confession of faith in Jesus Christ as the one Lord and source of belief" (Busch, *Karl Barth*, 226).

8. Busch, *Karl Barth*, 273. Busch quotes from Karl Barth, *How I Changed my Mind*, ed. John D. Godsey (Richmond: John Knox, 1966), 46.

9. Karl Barth, *Church Dogmatics*, trans. G. W. Bromiley, IV/3 (Edinburgh: T. & T. Clark, 1961), 101–2. There are, of course, other places where the issues of the First Commandment come into play, such as in his discussion of the unity and uniqueness of God.

Chapter 2

1. Walter Brueggemann, "Foreword," *Journal for Preachers* 26 (Easter, 2003), 1.

2. Those familiar with Martin Luther's *Large Catechism* will recall his beginning his instruction about the First Commandment with the question: "What does it mean 'to have a god'?" As the title of this essay reveals, it represents an effort to continue Luther's thinking about that question, only formulated somewhat differently.

3. The formulation here is not simply rhetorical. Scholars debate the particular force of the prepositional phrase at the end of the First Commandment: *'al panay*. It can mean: "before me" (in front of me or preceding me), "beside me" (alongside me), "besides me" (in my place, except me),

and "over against me" (in hostile confrontation with me). The interpretive issue is not choosing one over the others but recognizing and dealing with the fact that all of these meanings are present in the commandment: (1) You have no other gods *in front of* this God, taking a prior place to the Lord of Israel; (2) You have no other gods placed in a pantheon *alongside* the Lord; (3) No other god may *take the place* of the Lord for you; and finally, (4) You may not set any god *over against* the Lord.

4. For Sinai as a metaphor for the initial giving of the law and for its ongoing interpretation, see Walter Brueggemann, *The Covenanted Self: Explorations in Law and Covenant*, ed. Patrick D. Miller (Minneapolis: Fortress Press, 1999), 49–51.

Chapter 3

1. In the context of the whole of Scripture, Robert Jenson properly notes that this Exodus self-identification of the Lord—as the one who, in grace and mercy, sets free the enslaved and suffering—continues to be demonstrated in the story and has its New Testament form in the identification of "the Lord your God" as the one who raised Jesus from the dead (*Systematic Theology I: The Triune God* [New York: Oxford Univ. Press, 1997], 44). This continuity is also central to the ministry and work of Jesus as articulated in Luke 4:16-21,

when Jesus reads from Isaiah 58 and 61 and announces that this scripture about the Lord sending one to bring good news to the poor and release to the captives is now fulfilled in the hearing of those who are before him.

2. Stephen Dunn, *New and Selected Poems 1974-1994* (New York: Norton, 1994), 183–84.

3. Barth, "The First Commandment as an Axiom of Theology," 72–75.

4. See n. 3 of chapter 2.

5. See in this connection Regina Schwartz, *The Curse of Cain: The Violent Legacy of Monotheism* (Chicago: Univ. of Chicago Press, 1997); and Rodney Stark, *One True God: Historical Consequences of Monotheism* (Princeton: Princeton University Press, 2001).

6. Such difficult texts, of course, need careful interpretive efforts and cannot be handled in simplistic fashion. See, e.g., Nathan MacDonald. *Deuteronomy and the Meaning of 'Monotheism,'* Forschungen zum Alten Testament, 2/1 (Tübingen: Mohr/Siebeck, 2003), 108–22.

7. See now Ellen F. Davis, "Critical Traditioning: Seeking an Inner Biblical Hermeneutic," in *The Art of Reading Scripture*, ed. Ellen F. Davis and Richard B. Hays (Grand Rapids: Eerdmans, 2003), 174–77. The parable is not without its ambiguity about the identity of the neighbor in the question. He may be the one in need or the one who

responds to the need. And the neighbor may be the one who tells the parable and elsewhere speaks of being ministered to in his need as one ministers to the brother or sister who is hungry, thirsty, naked, sick, in prison, or a stranger (Matt 25:31–46).

Chapter 4

1. Deut 13:4; 1 Kings 18:21; 2 Kings 23:3; cf. 1 Sam 12:14; 1 Kings 11:6. The words of Elijah at Mount Carmel set the commandment in its starkest terms: "If the Lord is God, follow him; but if Baal, then follow him" (1 Kings 18:21).

2. Deut 6:14; 8:19; 11:28; 13:2; 28:14; cf. Judg 2:12, 19; 1 Kings 11:2, 10.

3. The texts are too numerous to list, but they would include Elijah's conflict with the prophets of Baal in 1 Kings 18; the Ark narrative in 1 Sam 4–6, with its climax in the temple of Dagon (1 Sam 5:1–5); Ps 82; polemic against the idols in Jeremiah (e.g. 10:1–16) and Isaiah 40–55 (e.g. 40:18–20; 46); and the courtroom speeches of Isaiah of Babylon that develop an apologetic against the reputed power of the gods of Babylon to show they can do nothing (e.g. Isa 41:1–5, 21–29).

Chapter 5

1. Cited in the *Oxford English Dictionary* under "mammonolatry."

2. Friedrich Hauck, "mamōnās," in *Theological Dictionary of the New Testament*, vol. 4, ed. Gerhard Kittel (Grand Rapids: Eerdmans, 1967), 390.

Chapter 6

1. *The Nature of Doctrine: Religion and Theology in a Postliberal Age* (Philadelphia: Westminster, 1984).

2. It is, of course, precisely this inflammatory prophetic word that has introduced the priest-prophet dialogue into the book at this point. The inclusion of the narrative of priest and prophet in the midst of the series of vision reports in Amos 7 is due to the presence of the word about Jeroboam dying by the sword in both the third vision report (7:9) and the story of the encounter between Amos and Amaziah (7:11).

3. See Patrick D. Miller, *Israelite Religion and Biblical Theology,* JSOTSup 267 (Sheffield: Sheffield Academic, 2000), 529–34.

4. See the comment of Calvin in his discussion of the Fifth Commandment:

> But inasmuch as the reverence which children pay to their parents is accounted a sort of piety, some have

therefore foolishly placed this precept in the First Table. Nor are they supported in this by Paul, though he does not enumerate this Commandment, where he collects the sum of the Second Table, (Rom. xiii. 9;) for he does this designedly, because he is there expressly teaching that obedience is to be paid to the authority of kings and magistrates.

(John Calvin, *Commentaries on the Four Last Books of Moses arranged in the Form of a Harmony*, trans. Charles William Bingham [Edinburgh: Calvin Translation Society, 1854], 7).

5. For the connection of the Fifth Commandment (honoring parents) to the statutes in Deuteronomy having to do with various leaders and officials (Deut 16:18–18:22), see, e.g., Aileen Guilding, "Notes on the Hebrew Law Codes," *Journal of Theological Studies,* 49 (1948): 52; Stephen A. Kaufman, "The Structure of the Deuteronomic Law," *Maarav* 1, no. 2 (1978-79): 133–34; Georg Braulik, "The Sequence of the Laws in Deuteronomy 12–26 and in the Decalogue," in *A Song of Power and the Power of Song: Essays in Deuteronomy*, ed. Duane L. Christensen, Sources for Biblical and Theological Study (Winona Lake, Ind.: Eisenbrauns, 1993), 327; Dennis Olson, *Deuteronomy and the Death*

of Moses: A Theological Reading, Overtures to Biblical Theology (Minneapolis: Fortress Press, 1994), 78–86.

Chapter 7

1. On the importance of the affective dimension in the love of God, see now Jacqueline Lapsley, "Feeling Our Way: Love for God in Deuteronomy," *Catholic Biblical Quarterly* 65 (2003): 350–69.

2. Louis Finkelstein, *Akiba: Scholar, Saint, and Martyr* (New York: Atheneum, 1981), 276-77.

3. "This is my comfort in my distress,

> that your promise gives me life."
> (Ps 119:50)

Psalm 119 is one of the most emphatic and eloquent biblical articulations of this total trust that is implied in the keeping of the First Commandment.

4. The theme of the Lord as refuge is so pervasive to the Psalter that Jerome Creach has argued for it as a major editorial clue to the shaping of the whole Psalter (*Yahweh as Refuge and the Editing of the Hebrew Psalter*, JSOTSup 217 [Sheffield: Sheffield Academic, 1996]).

5. Quoted from Paul Woodruff, *Reverence: Renewing a Forgotten Virtue* (New York: Oxford Univ. Press, 2001), 56.

6. Ibid., 57.

7. The conscience is taken up in chapter 20 of The Westminster Confession of Faith (1646), one of the historic Reformed creeds. See *Creeds of the Churches: A Reader in Christian Doctrine from the Bible to the Present*, ed. John H. Leith (Louisville: John Knox Press, 1982), 215–16.

8. Psalms 145–150.

Chapter 8

1. P. Lehmann, *The Decalogue and a Human Future: The Meaning of the Commandments for Making and Keeping Human Life Human* (Grand Rapids: Eerdmans, 1995), 101.

2. That is, they will say *Hasshem*, Hebrew for "the name," when they need to speak the name of God.